Memory WORKSHOP

Telling Your Life Stories

MEMORY WORKSHOP

Authors:
Barbara Shoup
Darolyn "Lyn" Jones

ISBN: 978-0-9967438-1-5

Printed in the United States of America

Book Design & Layout:
Andrea Boucher

INwords PUBLICATIONS
PRESENTED BY THE INDIANA WRITERS CENTER

ALLEN WHITEHILL CLOWES CHARITABLE FOUNDATION

WITH SUPPORT FROM:
ARTSCOUNCIL
AND THE CITY OF INDIANAPOLIS

INDIANA ARTS COMMISSION
MAKING THE ARTS HAPPEN

BUTLER | JORDAN COLLEGE
of the ARTS

CELEBRATING **50** YEARS

**National
Endowment
for the Arts**
arts.gov

Table of Contents

Introduction

Maybe you want to preserve the stories of your life for your family; maybe you want to write them solely for yourself—to better understand what made you who you are, perhaps to help heal a hurt that won't let go. Maybe you feel you have a story to tell that the wider world needs to know.

Memory Workshop invites you enter the satisfying process of getting those stories told. It offers practical insights about how writing works and a series of writing exercises to help you identify the moments of your life worth telling and find the voice to bring them to life on the page.

At the Indiana Writers Center, we believe that everyone has a story to tell and that telling our stories matters—to ourselves, to our families, and to our communities. Stories make people real. They help us see what the world looks like through someone else's eyes, what it feels like to be inside someone else's skin.

We know this is true from the writing that's come from our successful Memoir Project. Homeless women, incarcerated girls, veterans, senior citizens, farmers, victims of domestic abuse, and school children—most with little or no experience as writers—have written stories that have delighted, saddened, amazed, enlightened, and enraged us. Made us see the world in a whole new way. The published anthologies of our students' work have done the same for countless readers and, in some cases, have become an important resource for those in social service agencies that serve the writers' needs.

Few of these people were experienced writers, many had never written at all and, in the beginning, didn't believe they could. Some thought the stories of their lives were too ordinary to tell, but in every memoir workshop we teach, writers are surprised at least once by the power of their "ordinary" stories once they find the voices to tell them.

You will surprise yourself, too. So gather up your courage, pick up your pen or sit down at your computer—and begin.

Barbara Shoup
Executive Director
Indiana Writers Center

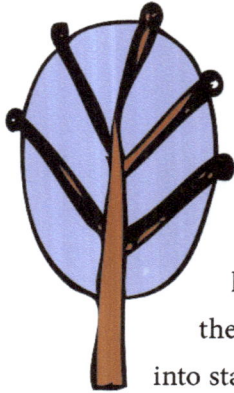

Why Writing Your Memories Down Is Way Harder Than You Think It Ought to Be

Say you want to write about baking cookies with your grandmother when you were a child. You see her so vividly in your mind's eye, her white frizzy hair, her twinkly blue eyes, her apron dusted with flour. You feel the touch of her cool hand on yours as she helps you roll the dough for Christmas cookies, the sharp edge of the cookie cutters that turn the flat surface into stars and Santas and snowmen, the glass bottles of colored sprinkles she lets you shake over them—who cares if you make a mess? You smell the cookies baking, taste them melting in your mouth, still warm from the oven, and the cold shock of milk washing them down.

It's all there, inside you. But when you sit down at your computer, or open your journal to write it down, no words come. Or the words that do come seem all wrong. *Why* does this happen?

Because you don't sense, see, or know in words.

It helps to think about what it's like to translate a story from one language to another. Writers choose words and combine them carefully to structure sentences with sounds and rhythms that deepen a story's effect. But a word in one language is unlikely to sound the same in another. In fact, every language creates a unique "music" in a listener's ear. The syntax, or order, of words is different, too. Ideas, images, idioms, and experiences in one culture may have no counterpart in another. So even though the meaning of words may be correct in a translation, they don't necessarily create the same effect.

A good translator knows it's impossible to recreate a story *exactly* in a second language, that you have to try and fail until you make the gap between the story in its first and second languages as narrow as it can be. Writing is a kind of translation; words are a second language to the heart. No memory you write will ever perfectly match the memory alive inside you, but that doesn't mean you can't write stories that capture the essence of moments that have made you who you are. It helps to think of yourself as a translator, doing the best you can to turn pictures in your mind's eye, the thoughts, ideas, feelings, knowledge, and wisdom in your head and heart into words. Get that first draft down, then try and fail at getting the right words on the page until the memory in words is as close as it can be to what you remember.

I Remember

So there you are: blank page or computer screen and your whole life inside your head.

Q: Where do you start?
A: Anywhere.

Here's how.

- Set a timer for 3-5 minutes.
- Write "I remember," then the first memory that comes to mind.
- Write "I remember" again, followed by the next memory that floats up. Keep doing it.
- Be sure to write "I remember" every time. The repetition of the phrase keeps your brain in the place where your memories live. Sometimes memories cluster: people, places, periods of time. More often they feel random. At least one of your memories will surprise you.
- Don't try to control the process. Just let the memories come until the timer goes off.
- Take a look at your memories when you've finished and you'll see that each one brings a vivid picture to your mind. Choose one, do the exercise again, focusing your "I Remembers" on that particular memory. Explore all the senses as you remember: sight, smell, sound, touch, and taste. When you've filled at least a page, stop, close your eyes and examine the scene of your memory in your mind's eye. Notice what's directly in front of you, on either side, above, below, behind you. Jot down additional details you remembered.

Now, set your timer for 20 minutes.

And freewrite. This means don't try to plan what you want to say, don't stop and think along the way—just write down the story of what happened in your memory as fast as you can. (It helps to write in present tense, as if the memory is happening all over again, right before your eyes.) Don't consider spelling, punctuation, or organization. Don't make any judgments about what or how you're writing along the way. The idea is to stay in the place in your head where you can see the story of your memory playing out, just like a movie.

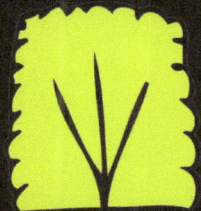

Keep writing until the timer goes off. If you get stuck before that happens, look at your list of "I Remembers," pick one and see where it leads you. If you think you're finished, you're probably not. The best stuff often comes after you think you've finished telling the story. If you have more to say after the timer goes off, feel free to keep going.

Remember, no judgment! Who cares if what you're writing feels disorganized or if your punctuation and grammar are incorrect. Revision is a part of the writing process: you can fix, add, cut, and shape things later. Right now you just want to get your memory on the page.

This exercise yields beautiful little nuggets of your life, told in your own true voice. Each one is a tiny first draft you can develop, a piece of the puzzle of your life.

Do it again and again. It never fails to bring up new memories to add to your story.

Don't worry about which memories are significant and which ones aren't.

Don't worry about putting them in order. That comes later.

For now, just remember.

Snapshots

Whether you've organized your photos in albums that go from birth to yesterday or you've tossed them into boxes and plan to organize them some day, they offer a wealth of visual information about important and ordinary moments in your life. You can use them to discover and imagine more about a memory you've already written about or as a jumping off point in writing about the memories they capture.

Each snapshot is the framework for a scene—and scenes are what make writing come alive. When they work—reading or writing them—it's as if a movie is happening in your mind.

If your photos are in a box, reach in and pick one at random. If they're in albums, close your eyes, open one of them, and let your finger fall on a photograph.

Look at the picture you chose.

Jot down details about what you see there.

Jot down details about smell, sound, taste, and touch.

Now jot down responses to these questions to help you dig deeper:

- Why was the picture taken?
- Who's *not* in it? Why not?
- What's the significance of the place where the picture was taken?
- Are there objects in this place that are particularly evocative to you?
- Did the weather affect the scene in any way?
- Did your mood or anyone else's mood have an effect on the moment?
- Were there tensions or conflicts at work in the moment?
- Was anything happening outside the frame of the photograph that affected how the scene played out?
- What was happening just before the photograph was taken?
- What happened right after the shutter clicked, capturing the moment?

Okay. Set a timer for 20 minutes and freewrite about what happened in your snapshot as fast as you can. If you're still writing when the timer goes off, no problem! Keep going as long as the words come.

What You Can't Remember

It's fair to imagine what you can't remember. Even the best memoirists can't remember everything. Do you really think Frank McCourt remembered every single detail and bit of dialogue from the Irish childhood he captured so beautifully in *Angela's Ashes?*

What matters is capturing the heart and soul of your memories: the way they felt and moved, the essential character of the people and places you're writing about, and the nature of the time in which you lived them. You can use what you do remember about a person, place, or occasion to help you imagine what you don't remember. You may not remember what your mother wore on the day of your high school graduation, for example, or what she said to you when it was over, but you know the kind of clothes she wore, generally, and you can feel the rhythm of how she spoke. You know what she'd *never* have worn, what she'd *never* have said.

So give yourself a little leeway. As long as you stay true to the people, places, times, and emotions of your memories, you'll imagine yourself into the kind of truth that resonates more than a simple accounting of facts ever can.

Show, Don't Tell

When writing about their lives, aspiring memoirists too often settle for telling you how things were rather than making you feel as if you are actually experiencing them. "The river cruise was enchanting," they might write. Or "My cousin Brenda was the most annoying person."

Assuming the writer's a reliable person, we'll probably believe him. But so what? We're no closer to knowing why the river cruise or his cousin Brenda matter enough to him to want to capture them forever. We have no idea what "enchanting" or "annoying" mean to him.

Good writers don't tell readers what to think or feel; they allow readers the pleasure of coming to their own conclusions. They identify details and clues that illustrate why they think and feel the way they do about their subject matter. Then, like detectives in reverse, they lay down those clues for the reader to use in putting together a picture of what the writers want them to know about their lives.

Remember translation! Notice how the description of the place below comes alive when the writer uses vivid details and strong, visual verbs to "translate" the general to the specific.

- *Assisi is an ancient and magical town, with beautiful things to see and many different kinds of people. I love everything about it, even the rain.*

- *Walking up a narrow cobblestone street in Assisi, warmed by the sun, I pass geraniums and petunias cascading from a high window, an ancient stone fountain, a tiny shrine near someone's doorway: a ceramic tile of St. Francis feeding the birds behind a wrought iron grille. A dozen or so scrawny cats on a stone wall feast on open tins of cat food brought by an old lady who glowers at tourists with cameras to keep them away. Steep stone stairs deliver me to the main piazza, where I find monks in Birkenstocks, nuns in baseball caps, townspeople chatting on benches, street artists recreating Piero or Leonardo da Vinci on the pavement in chalk. There's the clink of cappuccino cups at the cafes lining the piazza and the laughter of children. I stand a long time before trays of gelato that remind me of a palette of watercolors. Even the rain is magical here. The air cools, the sky turns the most remarkable deep, drenched blue, and the cypresses darken as if ready to whirl up into it. Then buckets of silver water pour from the sky, battering the pavement, splashing off the stones of the terrace— making the stone walls of the city white, white, white and shining.*

The first description tells the reader what to think. The second paints a picture with words, one that is likely to make her conclude, "Assisi is a beautiful, magical place."

Your own memories will spring to life when you draw your readers in with details that allow them to see, hear, smell, touch, and taste them.

When you've finished the first draft of a memory, freewrite about the prompts in the next two sections to help you dredge up more details. Avoid the temptation to think through the exercises rather than taking the time to write them. Writing is a kind of thinking—the kind that yields specifics and surprises that will make your memories richer.

Capturing People

Who are you writing about? Close your eyes and visualize the person in his or her surroundings. Sit with the image for a few moments. *Remember.*

Now set a timer for 10 minutes and freewrite about the person—anything and everything that comes to mind. No judgments, right? Just keep going. When you finish, set the writing aside and move on to freewriting about the prompts below.

- Write down three adjectives that describe the person you're writing about, then match each adjective with a specific detail that shows why the adjective is appropriate.
- Describe what kind of clothes the person usually wears.
- What is the person likely to carry in his or her purse, backpack, pocket, wallet?
- If asked to describe the person, what would people who know her well most often say? Would they all agree? How would those who don't know her well describe her?
- Describe his favorite place. What would he tell you he likes about it?
- Describe her voice, for example: shrill, well-modulated, loud, whispery. Describe her most common affect, for example: animated, flat, apologetic, hesitant, questioning, in-your-face.
- Describe the person's most common body language.
- Is this person plain-speaking, or more formal? Does he use fancy words? If so, does he use them naturally, or does it seem calculated to impress? Are they used correctly? Does he make grammatical errors? If so, what are they? Does he always use the same kind of language, or is the way he talks affected by his mood, where he is, or who he's talking to?
- Does the person generally think before speaking or just speak out? Does she commonly regret speaking? If so, why?
- Name one or more phrases the person often uses. What is he most likely to say when surprised?
- Does the person swear? If so, what swear words does she most often use? What words would she *never* use? If she doesn't swear, what words does she use when swearing might be the logical response to something? How does she respond to others swearing?
- Is the person funny? If so, how does he use humor when he's speaking?

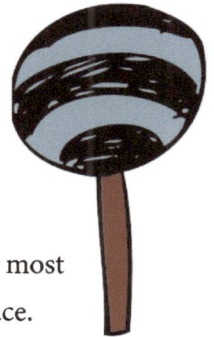

- What does the person talk about the most? Does her subject matter change from person to person, or is she always talking about the same thing, no matter what?
- Who does the person talk to the most? Is his conversation with this person different than with others? Is there anyone he refuses to talk to or avoids? If forced to talk to that person, what does he say? What would he say if he could speak his mind to that person with no consequences?
- Is the person likely to initiate conversation or only respond? Does she always wait for the other person to finish or does she interrupt? Does she speak more/less than others? Are there things she refuses to talk about or can't resist responding to? If so, how does she react if these subjects come up in conversation?
- What advice does the person most often give? What response does she usually get to it? Does the response vary from person to person?
- In what particular ways is the person smart/dumb/somewhere in between? How is this reflected in the way he talks?
- How do others generally respond to what the person says? How does this affect what she says and how she says it?
- What work does the person do? What are his special interests or talents? How does the way he talks reflect this? For example, computer geeks, sailors, doctors, mothers, professors, gardeners, and truckers often describe things in a way that relates to their work.
- If you were eavesdropping on a conversation this person was involved in, how would you recognize her voice?
- Consider the "music" or rhythm of the person's voice. Does she usually use long or short sentences? Are her utterances abrupt, do they meander, are they repetitive? Does she "punctuate" what she says with "like"? Does she use contractions? If she speaks English as a second language, how does this affect her word choice or the order of her words? Does the rhythm of her voice change because of mood or any other factor?
- If the person had a motto that described his life philosophy, what would it be?

Once you've responded to all the prompts, read through the freewriting you produced and highlight details that will heighten and deepen the effect as you revise and shape the memory you're working with. Jot down additional details that float up along the way.

Capturing Places

Where does your memory happen? On a lakeshore, in a French bistro, in your backyard, at a mall? Close your eyes, visualize the place. Sit with the image a few moments. *Remember.*

Now set a timer for 10 minutes and freewrite about the place where your memory happened—anything and everything that comes to mind. When you finish, set the writing aside and move on to freewriting about the prompts below.

- Make a map of the setting. Its boundaries might be marked by a city, a neighborhood, a street, a yard, a house, a room—whatever seems appropriate to you. Mark the spots on the map that have special significance to what happened in your memory.

- What landmarks did you notice in this place? If you were giving directions to the place, what would you tell someone to look for along the way?

- Write three adjectives that describe your setting; then match each one with a specific detail that shows why the adjective is appropriate.

- Write down several details for each of the senses you experienced in this place: sight, smell, taste, sound, touch.

- Describe the natural world surrounding your setting if it's outdoors. (Trees, plants, water, wild life, etc.)

- If the setting is indoors, describe the furniture, art work, objects—everything you could see, hear, smell, touch or taste there. When you looked out of the windows, what did you see?

- Write about something that has been lost from your setting, something that has vanished. Did it leave any after-effect, any ghostly imprint, or is it entirely gone?

Once you've responded to all the prompts, read through the freewriting you produced and highlight details that will heighten and deepen the effect as you revise and shape the memory you're working with. Jot down additional details that float up along the way.

Digging Deeper

Some people want to capture only the happy times, memories that make them feel good about their life journey—and that's fine. Others want to dig deeper, examine painful moments in their lives that they still don't understand, with the hope that the process of writing them down will bring insight, healing, and even resolution.

It takes courage to write about the hard things. You must be objective if you want to get as close to the truth as you can, and this means giving up any idea of writing for revenge or to prove a point. You must be prepared for the possibility that the insight your writing brings may completely change your understanding of the events you remember and the people involved in them. Something you didn't know when an event occurred, revealed as you explore your memories, might shatter beliefs you've held all your life.

Free-writing answers to the questions below will help you. Let your memory range back to the defining moments in your life. Look intensely at now. Pay attention to what floats up again and again, the way seemingly disparate experiences combine themselves. Look for patterns. Notice single moments, crystal clear in your memory, resonating down through time.

- What broke your heart?
- What broke or nearly broke your spirit?
- What scares you to death?
- What hurts you more than anything?
- What makes you so happy you can hardly bear it?
- What are your secrets?
- Was there some ideal time in your life to which you long to return?
- What is still so painful that you cannot let it go?
- What and/or whom do you wish you could eliminate from your life?
- What enrages you?
- What do you wish never happened to you or someone you love?
- What deeply offends your sense of justice?
- What about your own life do you feel that you will never understand?

Before and After

Another way to dredge up memories about the more challenging times in your life is to consider the moments that changed how you saw the world, moments by which you mark time. These might be obviously significant, like a death, or seemingly small, like getting your first library card. They might be terrible or wonderful. But they are always things that you frame in your mind and in conversation with "before and after" because they changed your life in some way.

Before my parents divorced, after my parents divorced.

Before I went to war, after…

Before I met the love of my life, after…

Before I moved to the new neighborhood, after…

Tension and conflict almost always surround these moments—they can be painful, even frightening to remember. But when you have the courage to confront them, they often yield precious insight into how you turned out to be who you are. Writing them may bring a sense of resolution and even forgiveness.

Make a list of your Befores and Afters. Choose one and do the "I Remember" exercise to generate memories surrounding it. Choose another one—and keep going until you've explored them all.

And in case you plan to share these memories with family or friends, be aware that a moment that profoundly changed you may have had no effect whatsoever on those who lived it with you. They may not even remember it. That's okay. Every single person's set of Befores and Afters is unique.

That's why they're so interesting.

A Few Words about Point of View

How many times have you shared a memory of an experience with a relative or friend who lived it with you only to find that their own memory of the experience is completely different from—even contradicts—what you remember? But you remember it so vividly!

The thing is, though, your mother or cousin or friend's very different memory of the event is probably as vivid as yours.

So who's right?

Nobody. And, probably, nobody's lying, either.

It's a question of point of view.

To understand how point of view works, it helps to imagine that each of us is born with a clear lens that allows us, for an instant, to see the world with complete objectivity. From that moment on, each experience grinds the lens so that we see, hear, feel, and remember based less on what actually happened and more on how our unique lens directs us toward certain details and interpretations, shaping our world view. *Nobody* sees the world in exactly the same way.

To complicate matters further, recent brain research reveals that our memories change as time goes by. For example, on the day after the explosion of the Challenger in 1986, cognitive psychologist Ulric Neisser asked 106 students to fill out a questionnaire asking where they were, who they were with, and what they were doing when they heard the news. Two years later the same students filled out the same questionnaire—and, in most cases, their memories didn't match up with what they wrote the day after the event happened. According to a *New Yorker* article about the formation of memory, "You Have No Idea What Happened," their memories were "vivid, clear—and wrong."

So don't count on the accuracy of your memories too much.

Push yourself. Interview people who share memories with you, see how they compare. Open your mind. Imagine yourself inside the head of someone who lived through an event with you and see it through his eyes. Try writing the memory as you think he would tell it, in his voice. See what you discover. Accepting the fallibility of your memory will liberate you to consider possibilities that may shift and enrich your sense of who you are.

Revision

Revising is more than just correcting spelling, punctuation, and grammar. It's discovering the difference between the memory in your head and your "translation" of the memory to words, looking for places that need greater clarity or more specific details, and identifying things that can be cut and things that are missing. It's about staying focused.

Think of those anatomy overlays in biology books that help you both isolate the various systems in your body and see how they fit together. First you see the skeleton. Flip the page to lay the muscles on it, then the nervous system, the heart and circulation system, the lungs, the intestines—eventually topping it off with the complete person with skin and hair and facial expression. Revising is kind of like that. You start with your first draft, the skeleton, and keep layering in more detail until the piece comes completely alive.

It takes time, often many drafts.

This is in great part because it is virtually impossible for you, the writer, to see how your words are working on the page. The memory alive in your head is like a crutch that gives the words clarity and meaning that might not be there for a reader without that picture in his mind. A good reader is invaluable in this phase; she sees what's actually there. She's not interested in whether she likes or doesn't like your writing or whether she agrees with your beliefs or conclusions. She's interested only in helping you see how the piece of writing works, asking questions and making observations that will trigger a list of revision tasks for the next draft.

If you don't have a reader who can do that for you (and even if you do), here are some ways of looking at your own writing that are guaranteed to improve it.

- Highlight passive verbs and replace them with active ones. For example, "She ran" has more energy than "She was running."
- Highlight adverbs and "translate" them to strong verbs. For example, instead of settling for "he walked slowly," delete the adverb and show the reader exactly how he walked by using a verb like "sauntered," "shuffled," "trudged." Each of these verbs brings a different, very specific picture to the reader's mind—and functions as a clue to the walker's physical condition and/or state of mind.

- Highlight adjectives that generalize and make judgments and replace them with specific details that paint a picture of what you want the reader to know.

- Avoid "information dumps" in a piece of writing, especially at the beginning. Trust the reader. Provide information only when it's needed to clarify what's happening at a particular moment in the story, allowing the reader the pleasure of picking up clues along the way.

- If you need more details but you're having trouble bringing them up, do the "I Remember" exercise again. You can also try the "Standing in the Image" exercise: With your eyes closed, envision the memory. Look straight ahead, noting anything you see, hear, smell, touch, and taste. Look to one side and then the other; look above, below, and behind. Add any new details that emerge to your writing.

- To find and keep your focus, finish this sentence about your memory: "This is the story about what happens when…" When you've done that, the focus will be clear to you. You'll know what the beginning, middle, and end of the story should be. Once you establish this, remove anything that doesn't enrich or enlighten the story you're telling while adding details and events that make the story stronger.

Writing a Full-Length Memoir

A memoir tells the story of something that happened during a particular time in a person's life or tracks a single theme or thread that runs through it—as opposed to an autobiography, which is a chronological account of a person's whole life. Memoirs emphasize certain life experiences above others, often those that challenged and ultimately changed the way the writer saw himself and his world. All of the techniques you've learned so far about getting down your memories apply to writing a full-length memoir, too—it's just a bigger, more complicated task.

Good memoirs read like novels. They introduce and develop a set of complex "characters," with tensions bubbling around them. They proceed through time in a series of scenes that are held together by passages of narrative. They stay focused. There's nothing in a good memoir that doesn't need to be there.

You can just jump in, start writing your memoir, and proceed on instinct, if that's what feels right. You might even get down a whole first draft that way, which would be fabulous! But if you don't know where to start or if you start and get stuck along the way, try the suggestions below.

- Finishing the sentence "This is a story about what happens when…" is a good place to start thinking about what you want your memoir to be. For example, *This is a story about what happened when my mother was diagnosed with Alzheimer's Disease and I went home to take care of her until she died.* Or, *This is the story of what happened when the abuse of alcohol, first by my parents during my childhood and later by myself, took me down a path of destruction but eventually led me to a sober, productive life.* Each one of these descriptions holds within it the focus, time frame, and arc of a story. Each one offers direction about what should be included in the story and what should not. Each one suggests a logical beginning, middle, and end.

- Brainstorm a list of scenes that you might include in the book. Let them emerge randomly, with no judgment. You may or may not use them all. You'll probably think of more once you begin the actual writing process. But the set of scenes you come up with will give you a place to start.

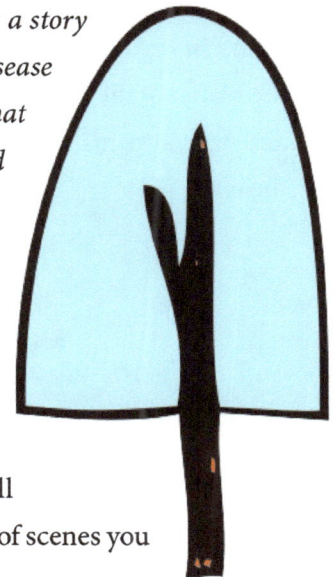

- Some of the scenes on your list might have happened during the period of time you're writing about; others may have occurred before it began but are important because they inform the period of time in some way. For example, if you are writing about caring for your mother with Alzheimer's Disease, memories of her from before the disease took hold would serve as flashbacks to illustrate how your relationship with her changed when you became her caretaker.

- If you're writing about an issue that's affected your life over a long period of time, look at the list of scenes you've written down and put them in chronological order (noting when they happened) as closely as you can remember—feeling free to add new scenes you think of as you write. Look at clusters of scenes in particular time periods. Notice where there are gaps. Identifying periods of time when the issue affected your life more than others will help you discover the right structure for your memoir.

- You might start writing the scenes on your list, one by one—either in chronological order or randomly, depending upon which scene seems most interesting and possible to write—not worrying about narrative transitions until later. If during this process the structure and flow you want for your memoir becomes clear to you, feel free to stop writing scenes and begin work on the book itself, writing the scenes you haven't written yet and any scenes you continue to remember along the way.

- Beginning as close to the end as possible is a good rule of thumb for where a book should start. Avoid a big information dump to "prepare" the reader for what is to come. Trust that if you open the door of your life to the reader at the moment it began to change, she will follow you into the story. Keep writing strong scenes and offer information only when and where it is needed—and she will keep turning the pages eagerly until the end.

↬ There's no rule for getting through the first (or any) draft of a book. It's almost always a messy process! Just get through it the best you can and then revise, revise, revise. ↫

Read!

Writers read. Voraciously. If you want to write a memoir, read all the memoirs you can get your hands on. If there's one you particularly like, read it again—and again and again to learn how the words work on the page to create its world. Ask yourself, Where do I know what I know? Where do I feel what I feel? Highlight the words that make the writer's world come alive inside your head. Study them.

Read what memoirists have to say about the process of writing memoirs, too. You'll find invaluable tricks and insights that make your writing stronger. The bibliographies below will give you a place to begin.

Memoir & Personal Essay

- Allende, Isabel. *Paula*
- Angelou, Maya. *I Know Why the Caged Bird Sings*
- Baldwin, James. *Notes of a Native Son*
- Bartok, Mira. *The Memory Place*
- Beard, Jo Ann. *The Boys of My Youth*
- Bechdel, Alison. *Fun Home: A Family Tragicomic*
- Brainard, Joe: *I Remember*
- Burroughs, Augusten. *Running with Scissors: A Memoir*
- Coates, Ta-Nehisi. *Between the World and Me*
- Cooper, Bernard. *The Bill from My Father: A Memoir*
- Conroy, Frank. *Stop-Time*
- Daum, Meghan. *My Misspent Youth*
- Didion, Joan. *The Year of Magical Thinking*
- Dillard, Annie. *An American Childhood*
- Doerr, Anthony. *Four Seasons in Rome*
- Doty, Mark. *Dog Years*
- Eggers, Dave. *A Heartbreaking Work of Staggering Genius*
- Fuller, Alexandra. *Don't Let's Go to the Dogs Tonight: An African Childhood*
- Gates, Henry Louis, Jr. *Colored People: A Memoir*

Memoir & Personal Essay (continued)

- Gonzàlez, Rigoberto. *Butterfly Boy: Memories of a Chicano Mariposa*
- Grealy, Lucy. *The Autobiography of a Face*
- Hamill, Pete. *A Drinking Life: A Memoir*
- Harjo, Joy. *Crazy Brave: A Memoir*
- Hodgman, George. *Bettyville*
- Jamison, Kay Redfield. *An Unquiet Mind: A Memoir of Moods and Madness*
- Karr, Mary. *The Liars' Club*
- Kaysen, Susanna. *Girl, Interrupted*
- Kim, Elizabeth. *Ten Thousand Sorrows: The Extraordinary Journey of a Korean War Orphan*
- Kimmel, Haven. *A Girl Named Zippy: Growing Up Small in Mooreland, Indiana*
- Kingston, Maxine Hong. *The Woman Warrior: Memoirs of a Girlhood Among Ghosts*
- Lakshmi, Padma. *Love, Loss, and What We Ate: A Memoir*
- Lamott, Anne. *Operating Instructions: A Journal of My Son's First Year*
- Martin, Lee. *Such a Life*
- McBride, James. *The Color of Water*
- McCourt, Frank. *Angela's Ashes*
- Min, Anchee. *Red Azalea*
- Rodriguez, Luis J. *Always Running: La Vida Loca*
- Santiago, Esmeralda. *When I Was Puerto Rican: A Memoir*
- Sedaris, David. *Naked*
- Smith, Lee. *Dimestore*
- Smith, Patti. *Just Kids*
- Smith, Tracy K. *Ordinary Light: A Memoir*
- Strayed, Cheryl. *Wild*
- Styron, William. *Darkness Visible: A Memoir of Madness*
- Urrea, Luis Alberto. *Nobody's Son: Notes from an American Life*
- Wallace, David Foster. *A Supposedly Fun Thing I'll Never Do Again*

Memoir & Personal Essay (continued)

- Walls, Jeannette. *The Glass Castle*
- Ward, Jesmyn. *Men We Reaped: A Memoir*
- Wiesel, Elie. *Night*
- Welty, Eudora. *One Writer's Beginnings*
- Woodson, Jacqueline. *Brown Girl Dreaming*
- Wolff, Tobias. *This Boy's Life*

Craft

- Barrington, Judith. *Writing the Memoir: A Practical Guide to the Craft, the Personal Challenges, and the Ethical Dilemmas of Writing Your True Stories*
- Baxter, Charles. *The Business of Memory: The Art of Remembering in an Age of Forgetting*
- Birkerts, Sven. *The Art of Time in Memoir: Then, Again*
- Goldberg, Natalie. *Old Friend from Far Away: The Practice of Writing Memoir*
- Goldberg, Natalie. *Writing Down the Bones*
- Gornick, Vivian. *The Situation and the Story*
- Karr, Mary. *The Art of Memoir*
- King, Stephen. *On Writing: A Memoir of the Craft*
- Lamott, Anne. *Bird by Bird*
- Larson, Thomas. *The Memoir and the Memoirist: Reading and Writing Personal Narrative*
- Lopate, Phillip. *To Show and To Tell*
- Moore, Dinty. *Crafting the Personal Essay: A Guide for Writing and Publishing Creative Nonfiction*
- Myers, Linda Joy. *The Power of Memoir: How to Write Your Healing Story*
- Spence, Linda. *A Step-by-Step Guide to Writing Personal History*
- Zinsser, William. *Inventing the Truth: The Art and Craft of Memoir*
- Zinsser, William. *On Writing Well: The Classic Guide to Writing Nonfiction*

Author Bios

Barbara Shoup is the author of eight novels, including four for young adults, and the co-author of *Novel Ideas: Contemporary Authors Share the Creative Process*. She is the recipient of numerous grants from the Indiana Arts Council, two creative renewal grants from the Arts Council of Indianapolis, the 2006 PEN Phyllis Reynolds Naylor Working Writer Fellowship, and the 2012 Eugene and Marilyn Glick Regional Indiana Author Award. Barbara is the Executive Director of the Indiana Writers Center.

Darolyn "Lyn" Jones co-created the Memoir Project with Barbara Shoup at the Indiana Writers Center and now oversees that program as the Education Outreach Director. Lyn is the author of *Painless Reading Comprehension* and the editor of the digital literary magazine, *Rethinking Children's and Young Adult Literature*. Her scholarly publications about both community writing and disability studies have appeared in a variety of peer-reviewed academic journals. She is a professor of English at Ball State University.

Indiana Writers Center Mission Statement

The mission of the Indiana Writers Center is to educate, inspire, connect, and support Indiana writers working at all levels and in all genres; to recognize excellence in Indiana literature; and to provide outreach programs designed to bring forth the voices of people who are not usually heard. We recognize the power of stories, and advocate for writing and literature as essential to a community that values clarity of communication and honors diversity, tolerance, and compassion.

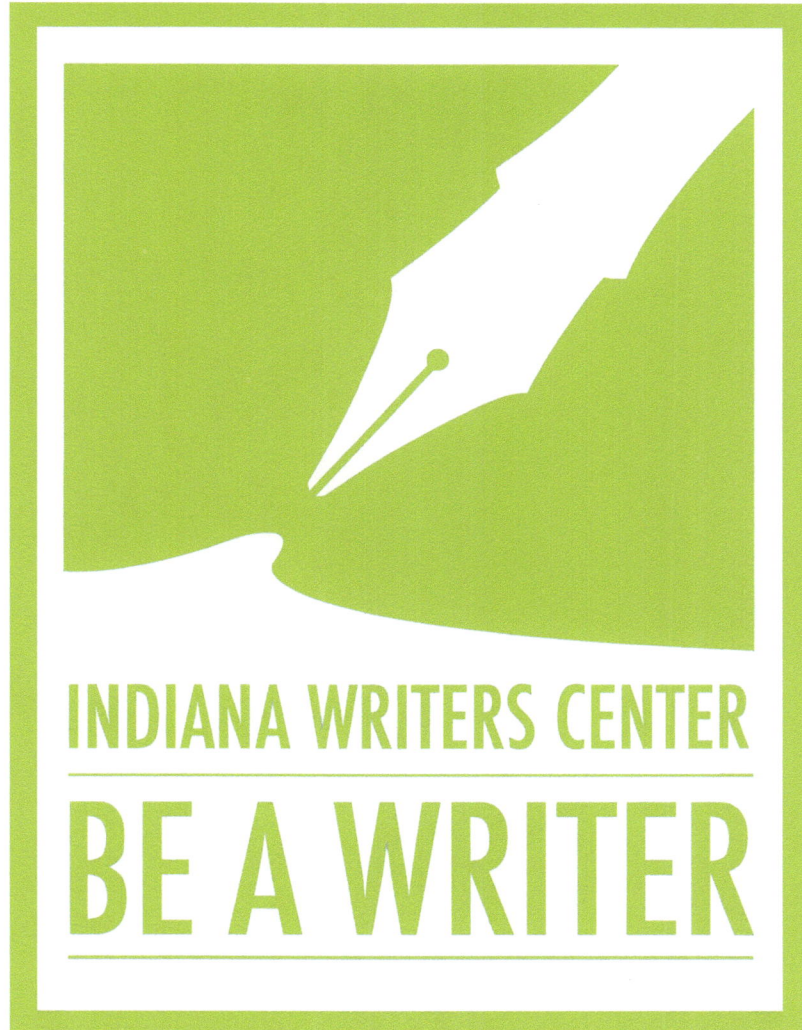

INDIANA WRITERS CENTER

BE A WRITER

Where Indiana Writers Find a Home
www.indianawriters.org

www.ingramcontent.com/pod-product-compliance
Lightning Source LLC
Chambersburg PA
CBHW061211030426
42339CB00003B/3